I0518049

Praise for Klyd Watkins

"Klyd Watkins invites us to be part of the American myth. Throughout the book, he breaks down for the laymen what being a poet means and truly entails. He speaks to poets and non-poets alike of magic, miracles, and angels. But what seems more important, almost urgent, to Watkins is what he calls the 'one and only very old song.' He often tips his hat to the various greats from the canon. He underscores the need and obligation poets must fulfill in order for their words to teem like ants, which may be innumerable as the poets themselves. Only an earnest yet lofty mind could come up with lines that have such bass in them. In fact, I hear a stand-up bass player fill the silence reading affords us with jazz scales that climb and descend in poems like 'The Nipple of Night' or 'Multiplication.' He is a fanciful and modest observer. So often in this collection Watkins' words (in his own words) work 'much better than they ought to.'"
-Bree Bodnar, author of *Upcycle*, publisher at Green Panda Press

"Klyd Watkins' poems start off with the speed of whatever moment they are meant to capture; they rush here, pause there, and, wandering as the mind wanders, find their way back, surprised and surprising, to favorite places. They are as hopeful as they are sad, as humble as they are pleased with themselves...Klyd puts all his concerns and his obsessions together with a sweetness and a light touch that are his own. His poems move along, keeping all the senses, as well as the heart and mind, continuously engaged. He writes poems that celebrate the spirit of one place so well that they show us how to celebrate any and every place."
-Stephen Thomas, author of *Journeyman*

"In this latest book, Klyd Watkins proves that it's possible to be both playful and dead serious at the same time. These poems indulge in his love of spirited language, especially in the energy created by crafting unexpected and glorious hard rhymes. There are sweet sonnets aching with rhyme, and there are narrative poems detailing hard-won truths beyond the veil of the immediate experience, in the voice of a survivor. Throughout, the poems hold fast to Klyd's declaration that 'I believe it is immoral to write poetry that is not earthly ... that is not earthy ... Guard against it.' Klyd is a sure guide to the mysteries and vagaries of a real life, fully lived, and his deeply observant poetry will live long in the hearts of its readers."
-Dennis Held, author of *Betting on the Night*

"The light rein on the method and the tight grip on the subject enables Klyd Watkins, when the young men get to the 7-11 when Rilke has to get out to let truth out to go to the bathroom, from where it has been sitting on the bump in the middle of the back seat, the least desirable seat in a car full of youth, to realize 'the truth must be along for the ride.' One of the most beautiful and useful lines in American poetry."
-Charles Potts, author of *How the South Finally Won the Civil War*, publisher at Hand to Mouth Books

"Klyd says in one poem that he sets himself a rule, never to let the poem tell something. If he's on his hammock looking at the light in the sky, the color of gravel or the growth habit of a tree, or if those things are telling him something, then he will let the poem relay that. The poem can do the telling for the sky or gravel or tree, but it is rule-bound not to tell anything for itself. Once in a while he lets a poem break this rule, which can be allowed because mostly he observes it."
-Denis Maur, author of *Man Cut in Wood*

THE WOLF CAN
SMELL THIS IS
MY ACRE

APRIL GLOAMING

KLYD WATKINS

©2025 Klyd Watkins
Cover ©2025 Abe Lara

-First Edition

All rights reserved. No part of this publication may be reproduced
or transmitted in any form or by any means, electronic or mechani-
cal, including photocopy, recording, or any information storage or
retrieval system, without permission in writing from the publisher.

Publisher's Cataloguing-in-Publication Data

Watkins, Klyd
  The wolf can smell this is my acre / written by Klyd Watkins
  ISBN: 978-1-953932-32-7

1. Poetry: General 2. Poetry: American - General I. Title
II. Author

Library of Congress Control Number: 2024951965

hammock hoy dia

Spirit Trough

Roy Acuff and Charley Pride talk about the
Atlanta Braves on the stage of the Grand Ole Opry
and other scenes

To Stephen Thomas, Charles Potts, and Dennis Held,
the gang at The Temple and Hand to Mouth.
They sweetened my survival as a poet.

"The sky allowed me to share its heart
Because it knew   mine was too small
     to give the earth the love it is due"

Rabia of Basra

hammock hoy dia

poems of contemplations in certain locations

2021 – 2023

hammock hoy dia — January 17 '21

I used to be telepathic with trees   Today for a while
I still was
Hello girls   I said from my hammock
Here you are winter naked
ash and beech   Ash I Am I Am and Beech is Queen
That's yr names, right?   The current that keeps me alive is
the same current that keeps both of you alive too   I want
to tell you
I admire your flex
toward sun   Light shifted then
on the spread limbs to thank me

front porch — late May '21

On my front porch I was
more interested in the smell of the night
than in what I was seeing and I
confused stars with fireflies and fireflies
with stars. One star said,
"I made the same mistake!"
"We did too!" several fireflies said
almost together. The stars
and the fireflies and I
were delighted and surprised
at this, as if we had just discovered
our mothers all went to school together.

front porch

Sitting on the front porch, the shadows of clouds
pass over the green field toward me
When they disappear over the house I smell
the faintest increase of moisture
That movement changes   Just now an unshaded
brighter green edge   moves toward me   Wave after wave
pass into me   I do not pass thru time
Time passes thru me   Time is moving I am still

The Wolf Can Smell This is My Acre

tiny cursive contemplation — February 21 '21

This hand   my pen hand   wants to climb
It wants to grab the branch above
pull up
and look around from there

The canopy   the tree line
is a kind of spirit skin of Earth
It extends Her sensory field —
Tree top canopy does this   Weeds too —
beyond her body like
our tiny white hairs   peach fuzz   laguna
antennae-extend us out into a fluid field
wavering with what will happen next among us all
with all our interconnections all rolling
forward at once together weaving
a world   and it's not just the people
oxygen is waiting to marry our blood

two hammocks, one with snow — February 21 '21 #2

In the treetops
    I've strung a hammock
        I lie there now

I strung that hammock
from inside my head
while lying in my actual hammock
in contemplation
    Snow lies
         in that
    physical
        hammock
right now
I see the white out my window
lying where I would be
if I weren't in the warm here
pen
in hand
    in tiny cursive contemplation

The Wolf Can Smell This is My Acre

Look back thru the window now
to my imagined hammock overhead in the canopy out there
in my treetop hammock
    Look we be there now
The blue sky blazes
because the light
        from spots
           of sun
upon the snow
reflects
           back up into
the sunshine it fell down thru
and that makes a crazy frame
for this sky's
ridiculous
blue

It feels very good
    having that blue
packed all firm within us
The blue that
means
to make us rich
directly

front porch riff — July 19 '21

A quiet bridge
to
abstraction and the blue sky spilled all over
travelling tribes of large white clouds

Are you here?
        Are you here?

A clown tips his white sailor's cap
above his moon
face   a head is drawn on his head

Quiet!   He knows we are here

now he unfolds his arm to bow
to us
Sad valentine hearts and kisses fly off him
and we applaud

We are left together   We look   each into the other
as if looking into a mirror   long and long   we look

hammock hoy dia — November 17 '21

Buzzards
    are flying way up there   today
I guess
the wind
    makes it easy   to soar so high
        and still   smell out
    what
they're looking for   With their black
gapped wings spread wide   almost immobile
tilting only   for direction   against the wind,
they are
beautiful
        But
it is death
they scout for   death
they need to devour

  Look how big I am   There's room in me
for the whole wide   windy
deep where
    the buzzards
reveal
  thru the slope of their gliding how
    the currents
      rise

front porch — winter '21

I am thinking I would not like
for my mind to be settled   thinking of people
the digestive system   of their thinking   so well developed
it can process just about anything that comes up   except
I guess deaths and births and various triumphs
and betrayals   Rarely it may take a few days to digest
something strange like a friend's political opinion
or maybe a very unexpected score in a ball game

but all that really changes is the pages on the calendar
The old memory battles having all contracted over time
down to where the movies of them zip pass in rumination
like a commercial   the long form or short form
of the same commercial

hammock hoy dia — March 3 '21

Buzzard again

It will be hard to spot
in the picture I just took
of the trees and sky above me
but now
her sweeping motion
calls my eye
then moves her over to the south some   behind me
   and out of sight for the moment
       while I lie
thinking.
Then her shadow
circles in the air below
the treetops
its two-dimensional form falls thru three
finding different surfaces
to darken   When it finds
in sections of descent
no surface to catch it
the shade alone
sweeps
       thru the sunlight
       close to my ear

Not just Buzzard
        the shadow of a buzzard!
that's some spooky stuff
            right there
It should have startled me, right? but on
        this bright day the falling shape
of shade thru sunshine
        is a beautiful surprise
    What we see   is
        the music of law

hammock hoy dia — May 15 '22

When sky sweet talks me

whispering "I turn to dew to form
around you"
Skin
believe me

listens
intently

hammock hoy dia — May 30 '22

owl transcription:

whoot
wheuuu wheuuu

ah whoot
  wheuu wheuuu

whoot whoot wheu wheuu

wheuu wheuuu whoot whoot wheu

The Wolf Can Smell This is My Acre

hammock hoy dia — June 3 '22

Sky
      tell me this
should I

figure out
      whom to forgive

or just go ahead
      and fly?

front porch — June 4 '22

Let's not talk about
Who the prophets are
And who they are not
We might get busy shooting
Each other

The holy one hides
Right here in the world
Hides in her radiance
And she may
Step naked out into plain sight
Any minute now   We can talk about
Who the prophets are   And who they are not
And we can shoot each other
Later   Right now
Let's keep on watching   in case
She shows

hammock hoy dia — June 7 '22

The buzzards
have not patrolled
for several days

I imagine
an elder buzzard announcing
"Death seems to have died down a bit lately
Let's just sit in the trees and fast today"

I notice their absence
because I've been trying to get a picture
They tease me   fly over all spread out
gliding black against the luminescence of sky
and by the time I turn on my camera

and get it pointed
they are gone

front porch — June 9 '22

Big wind   announces to nose   rain coming on

Why should this remind me
        once
        a girl
        came up to me?   At the community
        college   I was standing in a classroom
        door   She stayed in the hall   grasped
    my arm and folded it   squeezed
        like she meant
        to milk my bicep

I bet we all have once or twice at least felt that
        desire so specific and intense it just seemed
    acting on it could be the only right thing to do
    common sense to the contrary   Nothing came
        of her bold move and now
I blame me some for that innocence
But it's a nice memory

which leverages   just now   how sensual
to this animal I am is the sudden
drop in temperature
        the big smell of the coming of hard rain

hammock hoy dia — June 12 '22 — pronouns

"We haven't talked but the one time
before,"
Beech is Queen
said. "You know
I'm monoecious,
right? Why do
we call me Queen? Are you
flirting with me?"

"No, no," I answered. "God
is monoecious too

I call   'him' 'her'
          Why not you?"

hammock hoy dia — June 24 '22

Sky's
hands
take off
the husk
around me

hammock hoy dia — July 15 '22

When sky
sees she has my attention
she takes her clothes off
    A glow
comes off
the glow already there
showing
there   is more to show

sitting on a rock wall — July 29 '22

Beneath an aura of shade trees that
shield bicycle traffic from the busy street
beside it   near the World Trade Center
I see

sky
in her
mighty New York City dress

She sees I am in the wrong place
points at me   and waves

I admit I stop seeing sky for a while
  for looking at her dress instead   its details
how tall   we are in this city
     the rivers   of Manhattan eyes

couch poems — August 5 '22 #3

There's a rumor
the apocryphal frog in the well
is having a dream of himself
The ring of sky that opens way up overhead
onto moon bright night   That abstract silver
contrasts with the deep blackness he breathes in
makes it a bright black   There must be digestion
of that black breathing   He glows in the dark
in his dream   grows larger both in layers of glows
and in layers of the glows'
haloes

couch poems — August 10 '22

The writing of
poetry
is shot thru
with vanity
Humility has to win

a subtle battle
or the poetry

won't be really good

That observation—the way it's put—violates my rule
It's bigger
than just mine—Plutarch, Horace, Sydney,
MacLeish—but it has been my rule too—
that poetry can't say anything   A poem is a speaking picture
and a picture is a mute poem   Someone
or anyone
in the picture
the poem makes   can say something   can say   anything
even the gravel behind
The Woodcraft Workshop in the poem there
can say anything it wants

but the poem   itself
cannot
make a statement   See! here I am doing it again!
This poem
humbly
apologizes

front porch — October 7 '22

no fog tonight
almost
none
to catch the moon's light spilling

Instead
the dark
trees on the ridges and atop the bluffs
receive it   absorb it
But even with their massiness there's moon power
enough the leaves going gold are a different gray
than the green gray in the dark   whiter gray again
the bare rock of the bluff side   I look up
over the ridge top   Is
that Venus? or a passing airplane?   Is it moving or
standing still and jigging?

Sweep my sight on up to the flurries of stars
sitting here in my swing   my head in the stars
I breathe them in

hammock hoy dia — February 27 '23

In my hammock
I am
weightless   I am
up in the sky   already
up in the heavens
a little bit   I feel like
I'm Mr. Goodrich Balloon Kachina
and I am tethered
by cables to several points
on the fairgrounds   but
I am so puffed full
of something lighter
than air   I wonder   if I am not
lifting the town   up toward me

„,„,„,„,„,„,„,„,„,„,„,„,„,

One of the cables that tethers that parade balloon is

I do trivia quizzes online these days   Never cared to before
I do it because   it ties me   to people   I am leaving earth
and people   not just because I'm old   and I'll die here in a bit
  but
because   I am already
somewhat gone   and I do the quizzes   to maintain
some connection   Meryl Streep   won her first Oscar   for what?
Kramer Versus Kramer   Right?   See   we are yet   on the earth
together   Another

attempt at tether: I drive into Nashville To see poets   I try to
I drove fifty miles   To hear Khaos read   and when I got on
Grand Avenue   I realized I had no idea   where   Poet's Corner was

'You think you gonna
look backward   and see things   old man? The world   is turning
strange before your eyes   not in the rearview mirror'

Good thing   the holy one was riding with me   said not to worry
"I just   want to be part   of the world   a little more"

"you will be"

Sure enough   today   I went to the drugstore   and the bank
I went to see a poet friend whose name   to protect his privacy
does not appear   I will never tell   who it was   I had
loaned him a book by Sharon Doubiago and a book by Stephen Thomas
and he seemed glad to get them   Then   I don't know what
happened   what I did   why he got so mad   Before he'd had time
to read the books   a curt email   said come get them   out
of his mailbox   meaning   not to knock on his door   not to see him
just mailbox

So after I go to the bank   I pull in his driveway   and he's
just walking back from that mailbox   He gestures   with his arms
stay away   Don't talk to me   Cross old man   Points
at the mailbox waving his arms to run me off   like I was
a neighborhood kid who teased his dog or stole from his garden   As I
walk back   from the mailbox   books in hand   back
toward my truck   he is in his car   impatiently rolling toward me
like he's going to run me over   Like an uppity teenage jaywalker
I move slowly to taunt him and fast enough   for him to miss me

Earth!   earth!   Here you are!

39

Spirit Trough

poems of the harpeth river bottom
and around there

the mound builders

Where Mound Creek
meets the Harpeth River
Three years ago now I guess it's been
I looked across the river and saw the mounds.
Near The Narrows, I looked where Steve
had told me to look and I saw them.
Then I stopped at Scott's Cemetery
and read the Historical Marker the State
of Tennessee has put there. It says
it's been over a thousand years since
The Mound Builders lived here.
But I heard their flutes anyway.
That flute call, aggressive
the way some jazz players attack
the down beat with a burst of breath;
by my pickup parked in the cemetery
entrance, I heard it.
I hear it still, living here on the river.
Those boys sat on these banks and played
all right but the flute I hear is older than
the Mound Builders.
It brought them here. Centuries later
it brought Cherokee and Creek and later still
the Scott's ancestors. Even later
we Watkins came. The flute brought us all.

The Wolf Can Smell This is My Acre

We pass all these proper nouns and it seems
a stable enough world we can plant a garden
this year. But the fluid flute
furls out a flowing world that coalesces
and spreads apart at the same time.
Hear it?

on I-40 the other day

With my right hand I
adjust my glasses. With my left hand
I drive the truck.
With my subconscious mind I hold
the world together.
The sun finds a sudden span
of pine green.

burn pile work

my wee chain saw
Kobalt electric   just a pruning saw
really   I stoop and cut stubs of brush too fat
for the mower   close to the ground where the blade
will pass over   and I carry wormy logs
to my pickup bed   then on to the burn pile
an old man   finding himself useful   I hope
the mold doesn't make me itch
all night

spirit trough

The rock
bed
of the river is
a flowing thing itself, crumpled,
insinuating
onward. Above it the water
flows and above the water
air
presses the hills and bluffs that wall
all this flowing
and above that
spirit
moves   thru all the rock wall and air
and water, spirit flows, sweet smelling.

The river is a spirit trough.
I breathe it in.

landscape

Look around—we're in pastured rolling hills.
Here and there are shade trees for the livestock.
Here and there are ponds. One creek divides the scene.

There is a fence
the other side of that creek,
barbed wire, and across the fence
the pasture's grown up some with sage grass
and wildflowers. There's a little pond in there.
It shares the setting sun off its waters
back up into the sky and lights the air
gold above it, just a little.
The sun itself stands before a house, a house
you can't see for the sun, except
here and there its edges. Look back at the pond. Look
back at the sun, at the shining human there. She
has the same job Jesus had and Guru Nanak had
when they were here
but now she's at their house in the sun.
We see this from outside the fence, way on the other side
of the creek. We go toward the creek, toward the fence.
The fence is piety. On the other side, where the sage grass is,
is the lord. On the other side, where the sage grass is,
there is no piety. You cannot go forward
toward the lord without crossing the piety fence.

We don't know if it's electric.

holy one

Holy one I perceive you differently in the transparent air out over the field than when you pass thru the ridge. Holy one the waters reflect how we down here reflect back up your song and dance. You shine quietly holy one above the waters flow and over the bluff.   Dirt drinks you holy one. Dark dirt drinks you. You are first fertilizer. You furl the climbing sycamore out and the thick black willows just below the rock face of the wall. They shake, the willows and sycamores shake and you ride their forms holy one, slyly, making them barely bright.

shade of green

A flute
plays.
What a breath, what a long breath,
the musician has. His melody
swirls, does tricks you might see
an antique fighter plane do at a country
air show, corkscrew melody. The musician
is moving around, apparently, for the sound
comes from different directions. He is accompanied
by the tree frogs and crickets and uncountable
other insects making percussion fine
like salt sprinkling all over the night.

We feel we can't live up to the music. We want to love it
but we are not strong enough. We want to ride it
and it wants us to ride.   It wants us
to come along. It wants us to smell for it the sweetness
of the night. It wants us to relax but maintain our form
while it tosses us in somersaults up over and around
and tosses us up again just when we nearly touch down.
Before you know it, the flute is using our lust to green
yonder mountains. We guess that's all right.
Had plans for that lust but those hills
bear a wild beauty that shade of green in the dark.

it's always the past

It's always the past
Or it's just begun
The luck of the Irish
The lust of the sun

The sun behind a tree
makes the tree invisible
in a spot   Shoots right thru
The river tells its stories
to a changing audience as it rolls   Those
banks he passes later
hear the end and don't know the start
Those who hear the middle won't know the end

It's always the past
Or it's just begun
The luck of the Irish
The lust of the sun

serious valentine

Here are fifty-two kisses.
Go on and use them while they're still damp.
Affix them where you will.

four flows

November afternoon went down to the river
with the CD of Bill Chelf's electronic drone music
playing loud in my truck   I turned the speakers up
I rolled the windows down   I could hear Bill
where I sat up my Vanderbilt logoed folding chair
before the river

It's a long long note my friend is playing
It goes on transforming   It feels reliably
"here for us" this music It feels able
while emerging   into and exiting from
reverberant   flows of tone   taking color new places
then folding those places   the overflows
of overtones   swallowed   slowly   by smiling
silence   licking her lips   This foundational music
embraces the noise of a little airplane overhead
and the embrace releases as the plane flies on
toward Nashville   The two sounds stretching out their arms
to touch as long as they can   each pair of hands   grasping
at first by the biceps   then by the elbows   their grip slips
down to the wrists   finally fingertips pull apart in space   The music
flowing out my truck window is modest among the November leaves
by the river   So much green left   Nature's first gold is green
to turn the Frost around facing fall   The river's wet
flowing green   is award-winning   Most Fluid Green
and Greenest of Wet Green   both categories, it wins

The Wolf Can Smell This is My Acre

Twenty yellow leaves on top of the stream
flow past as the long note flows down around a bend
out of sight   Now new yellow leaves
appear   These too   flow before me   How
that note   stretches   on the water
Flowing's ever going seems never leaving now
Light dances with leaf shade   dances
by standing still   while radiant leaves twist shadow trails
every way I look   Now it is daylight is licking her lips
tasting the shadows   Nothing stands still
Light
dances   parallel   to these
parallels   to
the flute sound
inside my skull

I first heard that flute
like an auditory hallucination
in the driveway to the Scott Cemetery at
the historical marker there by the Mound Builders
field   I am learning to play
that flute   I can make it play
a trio with Bill's keyboard drone
and a loud muffler from a pickup truck
on Cedar Hill Road   The muffler's part
is in decrescendo now   as the truck passes on
over Chapel Hill

It's a pretty afternoon

by three

Everything is divisible by three
my mother. Nothing new can come by two.
The rock plus the water the run the river.
The river the fog the cloud wet sky
Sit trinely over rock ground rooted
globs of suns and you and dad and Jim
and me   Everything be definitely
divisible diversely by three

The Wolf Can Smell This is My Acre

at Willis's baseball practice in the park in Pegram

I sit
in a folding chair watching
fifth grade boys
practice fielding

on the grass with
its admixed clover
just beginning
to flirt a little

little mammals run around
in colored clothing   throwing balls
in patterns by bases to each other

            and the traffic over on 70   and in the streets around us
                  gets loud at times   and think how loud
that airplane overhead would be   if it weren't
        so far away
                Man is here

The only other presence that matches man in scale
        in my perception   is
              the trees
                      Plainly they
           outnumber us   they cover the hills
          above and behind the town   They get fancy
            in the neighborhood behind the park

The trees play
with pattern too
like our baseball
boys do
        tho trees do it
                standing still
 as still as they are quiet
past quiet even because
not only
are they silent   they absorb
     some of our racket too
  Quiet
radiates out from their hilltops

My great grandson just missed an opportunity to be brilliant
and I want him to show a little more regret
at least rhetorical regret

My neighbors and I sit watching little calculations run around the field
in jeans and t-shirts and baseball gloves   We ask each other
will the big boy be back?   and that little pitcher?

The trees are more interested in the moods of the sun

we live on top of ourselves

We live on top of ourselves

Breathe from a different story
than we walk from
Walk from below what we talk thru
On top of that   think   out of control thoughts
Over those   more disciplined thoughts
                Our "what?" is made
in many mansions   We don't know why
we said it like that

******

Beauty before me

On top of each other
the trees dance with their wood
and the trees dance with their spirits   with the spirits
almost fitting exactly
over the wood
They dance on top of themselves
as we do

****

We hear music
and move   Have to get
into the science of it
to understand music as "material" at all
Yet we do boogie to it
That less dense   reality   moves our bulk
in unison   one with another

We punch our fists   and shout "whu! whu!"
We speak a quiet "yeah!"
into the sophisticated
room

****

Beauty all around me

If we last on this dirt   long enough
I wonder if we'll   come to sing
as the Navaho sang   as they still
sing   as many red peoples
sing   What if it is the dirt teaches dancing
then   since   as Pound says   dancing teaches singing

this native dirt itself could eventually move us back
to where we sing like the Navaho?
These days
we generate genre so fast it could happen
any time

The Wolf Can Smell This is My Acre

****

Beauty before me
I see with my eyes
I see with my spirit
the trees dancing
their wood   See them
dance with their
radiance

while mowing #2

God is green
and smells like newly mown
wild onions

achoo!

I cannot write about the swans   the swans they are
so white

I cannot write about the man   who is
the source of his own light

The bee enters the hive to make honey
The bee enters honey home

This pollen business is serious   Our nose
likes it more than our lungs do
Achoo!   I like to pee
outside at night   What was of me
is of the air a second   as it falls
and then is of the ground   Useful molecules
all the while   Even our minerals belong everywhere
Just as our loves do

Klyd Watkins

this zone — sitting by the river listening to Bill Chelf #2

This Zone is the title of the CD
cranked up
on my truck's sound system
flowing out the windows
I sit on a log by the river
A fishing boat
rushing upstream
disturbs the river
peacefully   The flow
can rock so and recover
It stays calm throughout the recovery of calm
as the larger waves lapse back into the smaller

The award-winning
green water   The brown
pebbles shining
like gemstones
in this zone   In This Zone
the harmonics Bill progresses
are disturbed and are
recovering from the disturbance
It is fascinating to hear
My heart could unravel
the music says
Your heart, the music says to me,
your heart could be disturbed as the river was

63

The Wolf Can Smell This is My Acre

by the fishing boat's motor
and recover   It feels like this

I tell the sound 'thank you'

The music now walks faster   It has picked up
a drummer   The music now
walks faster   thru harsh-
er terri-
tory   It doth boogey
with a limping power   It fills
at the same time a color tray to evaporate
upon pardon   It nods its head at us
It patrols this zone
This Zone
can sing goodness like a Navaho
the human pitch breaking into the perfect
as an ornament upon it

Klyd Watkins

Beltane — White Bluff, Tennessee '21

1. before Melody's game started, the three- to six-year-
olds on the field

Pink shoes   pink
batting helmet
pink bat   tiny baseball
player
is told to swing
and she swings

Success!   tho she missed the ball
still she swung the bat   She enacted
the act
Swings again   Same success
Then the ball is placed on a stand
and she is told to hit it and she hits it
The ball creeps between the pitcher's mound
and the third base line
                              She is pointed toward
first base and told to run
and she runs   The fielders converge
where the ball stops rolling and consider
what action to take   One picks up the ball and
starts running toward first base and then
awkwardly flings it in the right direction

65

The Wolf Can Smell This is My Acre

The angles indicate our pink girl will beat it out
She will be safe

    2. between games

Hip hop playing on the speakers
"Young Geezy" they tell me

Bearded and in overalls a chubby coach
comes over to the steel-link fence
between the field and the bleachers and reaches
his car keys thru the fence to his chubby wife   also in overalls

I wonder should I tell them   it being the end of April
that this is Beltane after all   today and tomorrow
and they therefore must be the green man and the goddess?

Probably not   They'll do the job as well without ever knowing

    3. the main event—Melody's game

I intended to write some lines
on mighty Melody at bat—She
got a single—but

that had to wait
because Amelia was piling
gravel
on my notepad

fog

The fog

haloes

the trees. The trees
attach the wet
closest
around them
unto them. Soppy their leaves.
 This thins
the gray gauze
hanging right there
in the air so transparency then
outlines the trees' forms.
That's how
the fog
haloes the trees,
according to the muse.

+-==-+-==+=

The fog
is marching upriver.
Maybe thinks it's going
all the way
to the Cumberland, I don't know.

The Wolf Can Smell This is My Acre

\\)\\)\\/\\)\\

I walk
into the fog.
A kiss
settles on my face.

{}+)(+}}+)(+}{

The river
misses me.
When I get well I'm going to
put my rubber boots on
if I have to. Anything it takes I'm going

down to the river.

/\\/\\/\\/\\/\\/\\/\\/\\/

Now

the fog is starting to rise.
It sees some clouds it knows
from way back. It is
going up to visit.

><><><><><><><

New fog
keeps rising
off the river.
It forms
two columns.
Each takes its own path
across the bluff and the tree face
of the ridge.

+)**(+

The clouds
call the fog
up off the water
to join
the vast caravan.
Come on, they call,
We're going to Virginia!

The Wolf Can Smell This is My Acre

nature poem

i.

Sitting on my porch last spring
early in the morning as the fog was
burning off, the muse required

that I translate the barred owl's call.
Well, I said, he's saying, Sweetheart,
come hither. I have a hollow

in a hickory, high and dry. What fun,
building our nest there! Then
we will swap out some nookie,

yum yum nookie—yum, yum,
he is calling. While you keep our eggs
warm, I will bring you field mice
their back legs still wiggling.

Very good, said the muse.

ii.

But this gray morning
it is nearly October.
What's he saying now?

Okay, I'll have a go.

Sweetheart, if you can hear this,
move away a little farther.
Too many of our babies
lived. Too few voles did,
too few rabbits. With the eagles
having moved down to the bend
in the river, one of us
may live thru the winter.
Sweetheart, move away a little farther.

iii.

Along the fencerow, a woodpecker
roughly percusses an ash tree, stops to swallow,
hammers again. In the woods behind the house,
a crowd of crows, more than you normally
see together, have convened to caw
with angry, raspy voices their own
territorial allocations—maybe.
No—that's not right. Some
other debate's about
among the cranky crows.

The Wolf Can Smell This is My Acre

They could be arguing
mythologies, disputing the intelligence
of man. Whatever they're voting on
they don't
count the votes they just keep
crying them
over and over till they wear the other side
out. What are they debating?

The muse doesn't say.

Suddenly, a helicopter, my wealthy neighbor's, sweeps over
the house, low and loud, across the field before me,
crosses the river, headed toward Clarksville, drowns out
the parliament of fowls with whirling whacking of rotors
as rhythmic as the woodpecker's rapid working
so faintly heard inside the sky-size copter sound. Neither
of these rhythm birds brought the sun out, yet the way
cloud moves apart and sudden light flows across the field
you'd think one of them
did. Why, watching the helicopter,
do I think of Mohammed?
Peace be upon him.

There are two
contradictory
reasons   Both true.   Of course I can't say
what they are.

iv.

When the big air whapping has faded northwest,
and, after sufficient silence, the boy owl,

fathering forth, calls out again, the muse sits up.
Her ears align to catch his song. He's changed it some
she says. This time—the muse is telling me, this time—
at the end, it goes,
                                Hear me.
Move away a little farther. The eagles have moved
toward the bend in the river. Hear me. Both of us,
with fields enough, may live thru the winter. Move away.
Hear me. Stay where you can barely hear me.

The Wolf Can Smell This is My Acre

glad

Holy one how glad I am
to be a meteor that has entered your orbit
that burns now in your atmosphere
my ashes peppering down on your forests
on your rivers and fields

It was a dream, I guess. I remember

I was running. I called out, God, wait up.
I want to ask you, do you exist. He said, no.
I won't slow down, no.

The Composition

Passing Scott Cemetery, I see
three women
huddle   They touch
each other's elbows now and then
Sisterly smiles
break into laughter   They
are
at a particular
grave   The three stand
in relation to each other so the grave
is part of the composition   as if they'd posed
for a photo tho no photographer   was there
and I'm sure none of the four
ever even saw the poet in the Ford pickup
happening by

here

Holy one here
in the sun by the river
how glad I am to be your animal

improvisations — April 24 '22

Quit making it so hard
Ease up
            on yourself
Who are you defending yourself to
all day long
in that guilty voice?

It's all a lie!   Except for
being guilty of constructing
a sure-proof way of feeling guilty you

are innocent as pi.

.././/..//..//...//.../././/..//./

a music of speech
will reach   out from man

as long as man
can
talk
            he will talk sing too
if poems and songs
and rap and bluegrass recitations   if the Sufis
the Psalms and limericks and people like
Bukowski and Charles Bernstein   if they

78

all go away at the same time
for some reason well it won't be long
till something along those lines
spreads among us all over again   Flowers
bring bees we know but maybe it is backwards
as bees bring flowering   some need some
longing would pull song out of us all over again

                    /\/\\/\/\/\\/\

Everyvowel

Glowing like embers   frozen into crystals   such colors!

Everyvowel to the rescue!   Let the
London Bach Chorale join Lavern Baker in singing
Everyvowel to the rescue!
Everyvowel has us all soaked with certainty
And it's certainly
time   Everyvowel asks if all of this

all the stars' indeed the constellations' revolutions all the
motion
down to the little dust tornado at the edge of the river
dropping its separate body bits when the wind whirl resolves

Everyvowel asks if all this
tries
to wake us up
or does it try

to keep us asleep?

<?><?><?><?>

A lone goose flies over   just left the river
I think it wants some goose
over in a neighbor's pond
to know he's coming
Stay there   I'm coming to see you
Stay there
I don't see what else would set it out alone
so urgently honking across the sky

campsite on the river — September 30 '22

The river's jade flow   reflects   for example   green
hanging low
out over the other
bank   Leaf colors lighter in there   Lifting
and falling yellow crawls in one place   on top of the water
Wrinkling shows where the wind was   just now
levels when wind lifts away   Water

reflects
much
Can it be
the river is also   itself   reflection? I am someway
connected to the river   The water's movement
resembles a wide melody
that always sweeps thru me

Yet
to say   the flowing before me   mirrors
what flows   thru me   reverses
reflection's direction   since the yellow
on the water below
is
without mass   it essentially   and infinitely
weighs less than the green
leaves above it in the air   Reflections are less dense
than
what they are reflections of   we've induced that

The Wolf Can Smell This is My Acre

Logic   you clown   stand on your head   right out there   top
          of your head on top of the water   Seeing your
reflection
is right-side up now

        declare

where
that flute breath that flowing thru me stands me up
meets death halfway   we get   this
beautiful water

rock bar — October 2 '22

I daydreamed I had to be the sun for a while
The white sparkling on the water set me off

I got to choose when I took the shift
I could have beautiful October or—gasp—May!

Yes, I was tempted to go with the plowing months
and power cultivation and the planting of seeds

but I said
I guess around March or late February
I want to be the one to thaw the ground

The Wolf Can Smell This is My Acre

rock bar — October 3 '22

The statement
I am in the present tense
is
in the present tense

but not by the time it's finished

I am

in the present tense   I was
when the sentence started
and I have kept up

The river runs low thru
this day
        perpetually
    leaving   I think
   she
waves
back at me   the river day does   in her blue-
sky skin   and her
ridge side full of autumn leaves colored
brassiere

The best part
to breathe in   and digest   is the layer
just as it goes   Before
that beauty unrolling a current back toward me reverse
to the river's   to catch
each moment's   energies
I have to keep up   I am
that butterfly clinging to a stem there   so light
against the breeze   I must softly row my wings   to stand still

campsite by the river — October 4 '22

Who is here
with me   here by the river   What is
that presence   filling all cavities I see it
crowding up against everything oxygen
touches
                        I can call it names   good names
I don't mind   calling it spirit   I think its best name
is Nameless   In full   with the middle name in
that's Mister
Name Less Nameless   to you

but even naming it Nameless
names it
and names don't touch me   What is
that presence?

riverside improvisations — October 17 '22

The flute in my skull

likes
the river

To listen to the music playing in my head
I bring my skull   It brings
its flute   its multiplier flute   We come
for a silence which echoes
off the rockface of the bluff   The flute wants
that compound silence   That silence
accepts the flute's trills   like a schoolgirl's ear
accepts her date's tongue
in the dark of her father's driveway

  (*(*(*(* *)*)*)*)*)

The river reflects the melodies
of the flute   three ways I know of

One way
          the water level's so low
the rock spread dry riverbed
lies out in subtle bumps and dips and
jiggles and turns
in the shape of microtonal
variations

87

The Wolf Can Smell This is My Acre

and the bank   a few feet above   and wider
somewhat   nearly the same shape but
such different density   That's two

And the best   the shallow
bright water rushing down the center
carving the bed within the bed deeper

All three draw the shape of similar
flute melodies going on together   the river

sight sings me contrapuntal harmony

\</\>/ \</\>/

Red Oaks' green
goes red   I got a picture   White
Oaks' green   goes crimson brown

Death declares "I sure am pretty"

That time of year
thou mayst
in me
behold   These late oak leaves   about to crumble
sunlight spent their green and all summer's waters
making thru them acres of sugar   No wonder
the red and brown exits
are spectacular   The same
sun

has spent eighty years and counting
sweetening what was green in me

I mean
to blaze out too

at Ride the Tide Music Festival

Rainy morning   Campground
giddy with redneck
rockers'   sociability
We
are tribe   We don't
say it in so many words
but we know   we are tribe
How great the band was
last night   That's an easy thing
to talk about   We enjoy
meeting   we enjoy
knowing   other members
of our secret
nation   Slow rain
wets
the yellow pad I write on
The words above
blur where the drops fall

riverside — October 26 '22

I had to wear a sweater
today
first time since spring
The river
wonders
can it be
both
focused and flow
at once
the same question
all atoms'
assemblies
argue all the time   if I understand
what the scientists try to explain
And the answer is
both yes and no

The Wolf Can Smell This is My Acre

I say, the truth
there is no truth
bigger than the lie
is itself a truth
bigger than the lie   Not here you say
No it's not   I say
am I the vine
and you the tree
our roots commingled?
You say   sweetly

just now   you need to die a while

bottom field — late March '23

Brown
dried weeds all around but

river bottom mud
says

one pinch more sun is all I need
I'll put up spreads of yellow flowers
wee yellow flowers   here
and there   Just give me
one more pinch of
sun

The Wolf Can Smell This is My Acre

kid's baseball at the park in Pegram again

On the hills around us
the trees attend still the moods of the sun.

The green men and goddesses are
all over the place. Beltane
hasn't faded.
For example the boy   calling   balls and strikes
his face and arms   already brown   from outdoor work
here before summer even starts—
the distinct   and country   cut of his beard—
the belly shape   of a strong   but chubby
little green man   A woman once told me
I looked like a Wookie   Was she flirting?   Just now
I can see this neighbor the umpire   as belonging
to a species close kin to us
                    The spell
of seeing him   as other   lasts
until he answers his cell phone   and proves
in the chat that follows
to be a civilized creature   and a subtle one   too.

                I am moved to faint tears   by his service
to little girls' softball. The whole crowd
surrounds the teams on the field like they'd
surround a fire they were coaxing patiently
to rise into yellow red flame in the night.

Old men, we cry all the time.

The point to all this   is   Melody is in left field.

The base runners
know what they're doing   Someone has taught them

to tease
the catcher and the pitcher   taking big leads
off third   threatening to steal home.
The catcher and the pitcher   understand their responsibilities too
They continue to show confidence   mistake after mistake
Someone has taught them   The pitcher has a realistic
understanding   of her tendency to throw the ball away
so she runs the ball wherever she needs to   to chase
that runner back to third base.   This works
until it doesn't   Generally any attempt to steal   to second
or third   or home   will be successful   Thus each inning
ends after five runs are scored or three outs are made,
whichever comes first.   So a team that can get just one inning
to end with less than five runs scored will likely win the game.

"It's like watching paint dry"   one father says to me   but
I see he is intrigued by every move and gesture on the field.

The Wolf Can Smell This is My Acre

Again the point is
they moved Melody to catcher
and after dozens of stolen bases in the game
she tags out
one runner
My great granddaughter reaches thru
with her catcher's mitt slapping down
into
a new level of challenge   Strikes it open
for all of them

This new level they lift into is   of course
nowhere near   mastery   The cheers
are for rising deeper into the lesson   for
one step taken   in a process   that for all we know
may go on forever   for all of us

But this day   We won the game!

down here — another river poem

  Sing the dirt world   sing its whirl-
ing   sing its whirling   There
are
no
closed systems here   The oxygen baited
to marry our blood   Water returning
from the croppie's
gill
back into the river   The drunken soldiery abed   dreaming
of people they know and people they don't know
in the same   dream   There are no
closed systems here   All
be
mirror   The clouds
crossing the sky show off like pretty women walking
down a street   engaged with each other   Gathered they are
under the transparent canopy   of their confident conversation(s)
but
they are not a closed system   The "wait" light
stops them at the corner   A neighbor to one of them
waves   Those clouds on the other end of this conceit
dampen the air so faintly we don't notice the lift
it brings
breath by breath   even way
down here

The Wolf Can Smell This is My Acre

    down here
the only where   we can get
certain types of things
done
        where we can try all over again
to be good to each other
just once   down here
where love
[please imagine country fiddles   with respect   at this point]
where love must swim in a weighted
wet suit

down here   the only place
we can make the spiritual trick
of taking on a dirt body
                  work   There are
no
closed
systems   Sing
the dirt world Sing
its whirling

Late March '24

Cold and colder dirt feels Spring
flex inside night's chilled climax
fidgets to get fidgety

Not yet   means   be ready

Roy Acuff and Charley Pride talk about
the Atlanta Braves on the stage of the
Grand Ole Opry
and
other
scenes

Plato's tool shed

In Plato's tool shed
the plaintiff has said
there hangs a level level
as level as can be
in Plato's tool shed,
the one in Tennessee

Level is an interesting trick
in our curved world

leaves us as stacked
tangents
to truth

There is always room for space
When someone wants to make some
we can find it a place

The level said I'll go out straight as far as I want
and make the curve keep up with me
I can reach out straight infinitely
from here in Plato's tool shed, the one
in Tennessee

the nipple of night

The nipple of night is a black black brown
They were astonished that's what they found
The nipple of night is a black black brown

The nipple of night is a black purple blue
Lord have mercy, I'm tellin' you
The nipple of night is a black purple blue

The nipple of night is a gold yellow rust
Night knows she's fine   I saw where she blushed
The nipple of night is a gold yellow rust

cottonwood seed

At the moment
     I am
a cottonwood
seed pod
opening
in the wind
At the
moment
     I am
the silk's
first
kiss
     of the wind   I am
at this
moment
the silk
untangling
     separating
Already I am
     swept alone
up a hillside
     toward a pond
       but I lift
    at the moment and I
       lift again

The Wolf Can Smell This is My Acre

    I'm parachute
and body
    I am lifting down
toward the water at this moment
    I am floating
toward the mud
    Yes
touch me mud   touch me
there

on hearing of Charley Pride's death

Probably it was the early nineties
the last time I went to the Grand Ole Opry.

Bob was running sound for Becky Hobbs then
and she was on the show that night.

Two things about that night I hold onto.
One—Bob told me about this later, I wasn't backstage—
he was starting to go thru a door when he saw
Chet Atkins standing to hold that door open.
Out of respect, Bob said "not on your life; let me,"
and moved to hold the door for Chet, who said,
simply, "thank you son," and passed thru.

The second thing: I am sitting up in the balcony
when Roy Acuff introduced Charley Pride
and the two had a brief conversation before Charley sang.
I remember the whole auditorium hushed to hear
what these two men had to say about the Atlanta Braves,
their chances of winning their next ball game.

The Wolf Can Smell This is My Acre

Platonic Skeltonics

Pi and Psi
are bigger than I
am
yet we've all moved thru Birmingham
together   All pass mighty Vulcan I am riding on a bus
and the air makes way for us
π and Ψ and I

108

dump truck

One of those giant trucks
they have at strip mines to haul
dirt away Yellow and muddy
Too big for the roads   I don't know
how it even got here
It straddled my driveway and my driveway
is wide   Pulled right up
and dumped diamonds all over
my front yard

The Wolf Can Smell This is My Acre

your lost patio

Did you know there is a place
you can go
it is right by yr home
just go out another way
There is a patio there you didn't know you had
and the night opens in a new direction
off toward the northwest
It has its own sky
There is no anxiety there
whatsoever
The big anxiety about things that matter
is just not there   not even the little anxieties
so common we don't even
notice them   what a quiet it makes
when they are gone   you need to
find that door

multiplication

I don't know if Pythagoras could have counted all the ants
on earth. He was sharp. He might have been able to.
But with artificial intelligence today we could for sure
tho
even now
it would be damned complicated. Different-sized ants
live in different-sized holes. Some ant holes probably overlap
other ant holes, don't you guess, with the nursery rooms
of little red ants almost right up against the south forking
tunnel of big black ants, none of them knowing?
Ants are everywhere up here toward the top of the ground.
Who assigned them their job of aerating
the whole earth crust, just as,
for reasons that are less clear, she
commands poets and singers to blanket every acre
everywhere   with layers over layers   of verse   chorus
and percussion   of chant rant   rapt rap   elocution?
All these people seem to need so many kinds of songs.
Earth has room for a lot of ants   And lord knows
we poets keep coming   Here I am   one more   We keep on
reclaiming   for particular generations   and for so many
public secret nations   the one and only very
old
song   We act like
it is necessary
to make it ours   We act like we have to
always keep it brand
new

The Wolf Can Smell This is My Acre

arrogance, a sonnet exercise
>   (to a friend who told me I was arrogant)

When I admit that I am arrogant,
'tis same as saying I am insecure.
If I come on a' feigning fancy pants
that trait's as good as any other impur-
ity might signal flash from me. Be sure
whether I wobble or my gait grows strong,
while any wants, my selfish will, endure
at all, it's wrong to say nothing is wrong.
But shd I grow as true as the day is long
and shd my smarter teacher grow in me
till I be deep all day in unity,

then shall my arrogance at last unmask
and you can still pursue the wrong damn task.

a dream of two babies

David Pointer was in my dream, my friend,
the poet. We were on a lumber scaffold
against a towering construction project, a frame building.
We had ladders. We were trying to keep two babies
from falling off the tower down among
the wheelbarrows moving below. There was
a boxed-in frame and a triangular corner structure
that held the babies, but they squirmed dangerously
and David and I had to hold onto the framing with one hand
to keep from falling and at the same time with the other hand
guide the babies back to safe positions.

Then David faded off my periphery and I saw
I had both babies to manage alone. I called out,
"Hey! I could use some help here!" Then
turned my attention to the job at hand. I saw
that if I could move the babies over a bit
they would be on a broad board shelf
where it would be easier to manage them
and much safer, but it would require
two hands, so I used deliberate footing
and careful balance to not fall and both hands
to move the babies, one after the other.

miracles

Ovid was not at all interested in being in my poem until he heard Hawkman would be there too. Ovid—Roman poet who lived into the first century AD—he retells, in his Metamorphoses, classical myths, concentrating on the many moments of transformation in those stories, such as when Arachne, the champion weaver, is transformed into a spider and when tragic Philomela turns into a nightingale. He handles these moments, often referred to as the "miracles," quite vividly. Ovid was late enough that these stories are no longer entirely credible to his audience but early enough they are still an organic part of his culture. I think he matches us early 21st Century folk who can approach our super-hero origin stories as adults and suspend disbelief consciously while recognizing such reification as these figures achieve by participating in American myth. Ovid's miracles were performed by intervention of gods and goddesses. He was interested in Hawkman's take on the way our modern metamorphoses, of ordinary people into super-powered heroes, are always given bullshit "scientific" causes.

Hawkman and Ovid
drinking an ale,
Ovid said, Hawkman,
I don't know your origin story.
Well, Hawk replied, there's
little we can do about that.
The man writing this poem
doesn't know it either. But miracles

in our day are more mechanical,
or chemical, or nuclear. We do scientific.

I know for a while when I hawk flew
it was in a different valley and apparently
a different time. The people there

had to talk to me in Hawktalk because
I did not understand the people talk there.
I brought them rabbits and they worshipped me.
Then I would wake up back home in
Lenoir City, or somewhere,
just my man clothes on.

[The poet binge watched "Legends of Tomorrow" during the
stanza break.]

So it was an asteroid of course
gave Hawkman his hawk power,
his wings. Of course it was an asteroid
because that makes sense. The world
will get some magic in it. If they must come
by stories, Ovid says, meaning
magic's invasions, very well, but they will come
one way or another. All the pressure to keep magic out
only powers the squirt where it breaks in. The miracles
I told in my river of stories help us understand
we are more than human in our span; I make you fear
when the girl turns gull, she is still herself.

yellow Caterpillar

I don't know why
I hated myself. It was
somewhat fashionable,
to be sure.
At any rate, I remember driving
on the interstate highway loop
one day in Nashville
in a white '69 Barracuda,
thinking
I hate myself
and I remember
realizing
the futility
the stupidity
of hating myself. Then I thought
I hate myself for hating myself
and that opened
awesome
potential
exponentially widening
vistas for self-hatred, as if there were
an off ramp beside me spiraling away
thru empty space further than the eye cd see.

          But
then
I thought
wait a goddamn minute here.
I may have to hate myself but I'll be damned
if I'm going to hate myself
for hating myself. I don't
have to do that.
I remember
an eighteen-wheeler
hauling a Caterpillar
passed me
at that moment,
that moment when, I know now,
I started slowly
getting better.

a speculative contemplation

In the 4th
            dimensional
                        view
shapes have position
            not at one spot but
            at any spot within a swoop.
This blurs somewhat and variously locates
   the shape
            responsible for filling
all those positions;
masses and edges, or, for example, spots
where isolated light glows,
   all
   must unfold like flower petals in
all directions outward from their central image.
They must stack in front of and behind
one another. More depth makes it possible:
2 times 2, to make a 4th
   dimension—not 2 plus 1, to make
      our customary 3. The new   depth drawer
adds enough space for everything to be multiple.
The stillness appears to own
   motion,
      and if time
passes, any at all, things
      wd have to tumble, but time holds
all still, all everywheres at once.

two silly rimes

How much
energy a poem can store   It depends on the bore
No one and everyone are both keeping score
It depends on the powder and the pressure and the fissure
but most of all and some of you will complain
it depends on the little boy who lives in the lane

=+=+=+=+ +=+ =+

A tried and true official car
is parked tonight behind the bar
The mystery's what they are doing there
That girl on the corner I declare
Looks like the one that went with Ted
Before the cellphone call went dead
Perhaps they came to hear the band
To boogie backwards the best they can
And execute the executive plan
But that's a lot of trouble man

The greatest poet who ever lived was almost discovered

It was all typed up neatly. Someone had lovingly prepared it
for the world, or for a cousin, or whatever,
and somehow it got stacked on a shelf where cleaning supplies
were stored, in a medical laboratory, where it sat
for years, a manuscript that would edge out Shakespeare,
Whitman, Rumi, Rilke, even Basho, even
Emily. Add Rabia to Rimbaud—imagine—
and it wouldn't be any better than the verse
in this lost pile.
The janitor thought it above his paygrade
to throw it out, and he looked at it now and then
and liked to read it. It's strange! he praised.
One day a professor
came to see the janitor
to buy some pot. He was a hot shot professor,
edited anthologies, a gatekeeper to the canon.
What's this? he asked the janitor
and picked it up and began to read. He got excited.
He recognized what he had, but he argued
with himself. It can't really be this good.
But it is, I think it is, he answered. Then his phone rang,
and he seemed excited by the call, and as he'd already
paid the janitor, he waved at him and left.

It's none of our business what the phone call was about, but
one thing led to another and for years the professor
forgot all about the manuscript on the supply closet shelf.
Then one night he dreamed strangely. He was drafting a study,
or lecture notes—in the dream now it was one and now
the other—about a text of poetry, which he perceived
combined the essence of Ralph Waldo Emerson with
the street clout of Charles Bukowski. "And it works much better
than it ought to." That sentence his dream presented
straight to his graduate students. One of them asked
"Who is this poet?" For a second or two the dreamer
felt a slight panic; he didn't remember who the poet was
he was explicating. But the dream showed him,
discreetly, the name on the front page of the manuscript
on the janitor's shelves, the font, then, in that font, the words
from one of the pages. He understood
how those words were working because the dream lecture
was brilliant. He woke up and was restless
for the rest of the night. He fretted to remember
the lines in the dream, as they'd come and go.
And the next morning he called the janitor early
but that phone number was discontinued. Then he hurried
to the clinic, but the building had been torn down.
Oh yeah, he remembered now, looking at the backhoe there,
the building had been torn down.

sonnet — in candy sensual silence
(for sweet Emily and the judge)

In candy sensual silence, breath and sighs
are louder than their sweet whispering. "Stay."
"I can't." "Come back." "Okay." "May I?" "You may."
So quietly they speak they must listen with their eyes.
When either wins a tug, a kiss is prize.
The secret they create creates this space.
Here their love can breathe, the only place.
Here the merger of auras disborders strong guise
bodies separating know. And when
for real she leaves, the theycloudblend
tears and some must go with her and some
with him. That way until the next time come
he feels her with him anywhere he goes,
her smiling hoards his musk within her nose.

words can only beat about the truth, the holy one said

We say "beat around the bush" we mean someone deliberately
fails to hit the truth square on and only pokes around it, perhaps
to obfuscate

"Words can only beat about the truth" shifts the saying to   that's the best
even the most deliberate and sincere truth-seeking language   can do

I like that saying because that impotence of language is
what opens up the horizon where poets play   That words
can only beat around the truth makes poets kind of necessary
down here   But we can get to the point where beating around
the point is the point   If we think we notice we are closest
when farthest away   we might get goofy   It happens
We turn straight to the fun of failing like fireworks fading color streaks
turned prematurely smoke trail on the dark

Poets can get to where we are not thinking of truth
any more than an action movie is thinking of truth   we riff
for fun   and to show off   But you know what?

The Wolf Can Smell This is My Acre

Truth still must be along for the ride
still has to be in the car
    Truth won't be the driver or even riding shotgun but
even sitting on the hump center in the back seat and
saying next to nothing on the drive   truth has got to be along
or there's nothing there   not even nothing   At the 7-11 one time
they let truth out to go pee   It was awkward   Rilke
had to open the back door and get out and stand up to let truth out and
Rilke held the door letting him out   and when truth got out
the car was no longer there   yall remember that

Barn

There is a barn
with no door, or maybe
the door was designed to camouflage
and disappear into the wall when
closed, as it would be now, if it exists.
The only apparent entrance is
the   square on the bottom
triangle on top   hole in the wall up under
the overhanging roof, big
dark hole a hay fork could enter
and the dark of the inside
of the barn can exit there, or hang
just inside right at the hole
ready to exit when the night
signals. More dark comes out
some nights than others. Barns mostly
have dirt floors, as you know. This barn
just goes down in a rectangular hole
thru the dirt all the way to China. In China
there has to be an upside down
barn the same size as this one
on the other end of the hole. This
is the way the moon whispers
to earth—its radiance
invades the barn dark
thru the hayfork window and rides

it down into earth's middle
where the flecks of shining collide
with the lucid wet metals streaming
and steaming there and the scent
of the flowing rock in earth's core
hitches onto the rising dark
and goes moonward, whispering
something back, whispering something
black. Going up and down,
or down and up, to China and back,
doesn't matter the scented dark knows
just how fast it needs to move to be on time
when the moon will be on one end
or the other to be released
with momentum out the hayfork window
dark streaking out of the barn straight up
to meet the moon.

yall allow me to be silly

Yall allow me to be silly
I want to jazz a bit I got
a need for it Need to
I'm telling you tell things
What it is the bird sings
How angels form in negative
space where matter is not around leaves
where leaves are not among limbs where
limbs are not
  angels are drawn
around empty
air with the trees or the clouds
or whatever is there

Actual angels move into the spaces and use them
for form Clouds edge up against angels' crotches
like dirty dancers You've seen that above the looping black lines
that tie tall wooden crosses together along the bottom of the sky

Angels must be almost still They only have time to wink
For their visibility to move
the things around them have to move
because their skin their surface is where the nothing is
    and if everything around them doesn't move together in a very
coordinated manner these angels stretch and distort tho
that doesn't hurt

The Wolf Can Smell This is My Acre

Not really   Of course yall understand
I know very little
about angels   I am just being silly   just riffing   just practicing
fast typing   so if you seriously need to know about angels
        you need to go somewhere else but I am serious about
the nothing
 We need the nothing   Everybody knows without nothing
we are nothing
I am not here for truth directly   but I do need
to intrigue you and I can't intrigue too long
without some trooth
Just not too much of it   So I tell you
things about angels I don't know for sure just to keep talking
but I have the nothing in here too and when you hear the nothing
you listen with a second anticipation for the nothing pulls you
like a black hole pulls   No   less than that   but
like a twentieth-century apartment store pneumatic tube
one specialized with lube

Big white cloud Casey at the bat angel
took a crack at that angle   knocked the black hole
out of the park   out into the dark

This is just jive   just a lark
Well, I started out with rime   and then I quit
We brought it full circle   Got back to it
but when you see angels' angles flat
nothing likes it a lot to dance like that
with the seed inside   Nothing is a maraca   all made
of rawhide   has sun seed shaking   shaking inside

Nothin's   a maraca   unmade of rawhide   has
sun seed shaking   shaking inside   has sunseed shaking
shaking inside

I am now thinking in motion about
what
inside nothing   pulls seeds and suns
where to come

]□□□□□□□□□[

I used to go chasing my tail
I'd circle and circle around
When I used my foot for a rail
When I felt the root of sound
When I felt for the root of sound
again, when I rode the wind, when
the sky came kissing color on me
in me   when they win me   any
more   cause I roll on the floor   breathing
now breathing
of the music
man
breathing of the music man

¬(+_)(+_)(+_)()(_+)(+_)(+_)

in what room

In what room
do we sit with matter and mind
and the fire in the fireplace in the middle?
The flames dance a silent music.
The fire listens to what we say. Because we know
that it listens we are smarter in what we say.
It pulls smart things out of our brains, things we needed to know,
things joyful to realize. Comes a time
however when mind or something very much like it must stand up,
turn its back to the fire, and do arithmetic
while the warm air round us holds our forms,
in what room?

I am a feminist but

(written well before the 2024 election)

don't ask me to stop loving titties
I don't know how

I'm sorry   That semi-antimetabole
jumped in front of me

when I meant to type
"I'm not a feminist but"

I was typing that to gratefully observe that
We don't have to hear that
As much as we did a few years ago

Well it was a little irritating to me
because you want to say, lady,
why the hell aren't you a feminist

Still   what she was saying   was
I am not a feminist   but I claim   I should be treated
as the feminists say I should   and

The Wolf Can Smell This is My Acre

in the end that was
perhaps as effective   Truth is so strong
it is denied
only   by proxy   Yall are still wrong
the MAGA hats say   See   how we're giving
all these jobs to women
and they are   good jobs many of them   you have to admit
bosses   bosses of companies   bosses of states   of countries
We take losses   we liberals   achieving what we want

Many of those boss women   are Republicans   they aren't
feminists but . . .

Clarence Thomas
comes along saying not to protect
black peoples' right to power   Too late Clarence   Truth
has caught hold on the issue   We begin
to forget it was ever argued   We begin to argue it was never
argued   The attitudes we advocate
insinuate into the culture   But we are blamed
we liberals   woke folk   blamed
with just about everything

Really, it's a good deal when you think on it

And now there is a market for contributions
from women   adding Power to their powers

maybe just in time

It is fun to read Gertrude Stein sometimes

Of sweet music
drink us a Stein

In this mirror of language this glass I hold
the saying is a song   lift it to your lips up   the saying is a song

Saying the
saying is a song is a song   The opposite
of
l a n g u a g e   Saying the saying is a song

says something   The song is saying something   Lift it to your
lips up
The something
it is saying it is saying in the mirror the saying is a song

><>><>><>><>

Not all pain pulls at your masochist
They are particular   Pain needs
some structure to it   so it can be built on
Its complaints   can stack up one over the other
with parallels within the levels to strengthen the piling
like the holes and stems Legos lock with
That kind of pain can pull you in and shepherd personality

The Wolf Can Smell This is My Acre

I read that skunks have a strong sense of smell

Masochist when you tell that stacking sort of pain bye
its eyes still know they are beautiful

:{}:{}:{}:{}:

But yes, there is a gain of mental
energy when you break language
free from meaning   There is fun in the freedom
in the novel spaces it can spin nothing till it can
leverage something otherthan
and you get to keep the spin the sport of it
keep it going   it can't help but have holiness but it hides
its own tracks so no charges are brought

You still have structures to suture random vocabularies to build
not stuffs
and keep them in your treasury   put them on the whatnot shelf
with a tiny Lewis Carroll doll
                                          Then in addition
you can abandon the structures and have not even
syntaxial pattern
to where it is empty even of John Cage's
smile and we admire that

but Gertrude turns it back around
her abstractest
lines mean
simplest sweet
          things

Toasted Suzie
   Is my ice cream
Indeed !

            That sounded so abstract to me when I first read it
            I loved that abstraction

            That's the least abstract line I ever read

All I knew of the poet that night   Jackson Mac Lowe
        was that the same series of poetry readings at Cheekwood
had had Robert Creeley the month before   so I figured this guy'd
be worth hearing too and I heard there then
how his mouth music
was word-based because his expensive voice
was busy avowing its own
un importance and the un importance   of the delivery because
            the non-meaning of the word groupings was the event

there in the verdant twilit garden   There were six or seven other guys
listening to him too and I was wondering why I kept thinking
of Gertrude Stein because I remember I kind of wanted something
to think about other than how hard Linda wd break out laughing
if she were here hearing this   I started to grin when I thought that
and grinning wd be rude so instead I rushed again
to wonder why I was thinking of Gertrude

I got into it some   It was like thinking doing a strip tease   and its nipples
kept receding

The Wolf Can Smell This is My Acre

I learned when he was thru reading
that the poem I'd just heard
had been composed
   by taking Gertrude Stein's vocabulary from certain works
and randomly regenerating spews of those words
re-ordered   or is it re-unordered?

She could have done it on her own
   Instead—
   We eventually notice—she makes reality dance to her own
childish tune

It is fun to read Gertrude Stein sometimes

Ovid eagle bird song

I'm an Ovid Eagle bird
The fall is my fiercest flight
I fly down to Denslaw Town
To look in the windows bright
Hey Juanita Ho Juanita   Give a boy a chance
Oh Juanita Hey Juanita   I need to see you dance

I was walking in my man-suit
Once down in Denslaw Town
Past a tavern on the south side
I went in and sat me down
Hey Juanita Ho Juanita   Give a boy a touch
Don't you wonder   Like I wonder
How can it cost so damn much?

There's an updraft
Now and then
Up above the riverbed
It can lift me   thru the dust clouds
Into light up overhead
Hey Juanita Ho Juanita   I guess I need you to know
Hey Juanita Oh Juanita   I need to see you glow

The Wolf Can Smell This is My Acre

dream power

I dreamed last night   I was in a town   maybe for
a convention   I come out of a motel   It's night
The bed's pleasant memory vaguely trails behind me
toward my room   The wide white Southern front's
all lit up   And I call   mother   My mother died in 2008
so I am   a younger man here   but I had a cellphone anyway
Dream power   And that phone   when I tell it   to call mother
in its polite   feminine   voice   said   "you don't have
a [pause] mother [pause]   as a contact"   I looked at the phone
Wee light bulbs the wrong color   Someone else
must have my phone   and this is theirs   I wondered
where I was   and how I'd find mother

                    * * *

I don't know what to think about it   I am as always
in awe of dream landscape power   how it can make moon
cover an Indiana barn and illuminate a field of corn stubs
brightly right up to the triangle of barn shadow
darkening inward   climaxing as it enters the barn door
in motion   packing the hallway ever blacker   Or how
that same dream geographer makes city streets   makes them
meet   and   with every house unique   extend down
the hills   and up them again   every shrub
in place   You've seen that I bet

* * * *

You know
Another thing I could mention
I was reading
karl kempton this week   some lines
about the Mother   an Indian spiritual figure   I gather
A yogi I bet   Maybe a woman who knows she's
an avatar of night   unlike the rest of us ladies
    who've forgotten that   I remember reading karl   thinking
I've heard of her I think
 before   somewhere but   I don't really know
 about this   Mother

* * *

    Since then a friend told me she was an important figure
in Aurobindo's ashram, a French woman he said.
He told me this when we strayed from our conversation
about the game the Titans just lost to the Bengals.
karl's reference had had the power to invade a dream
and steer it so a telephone told me I didn't know
The Mother   but I didn't know whose mother
it was I didn't know   Didn't know whose phone
told me   Then   days later   this dream's   still sitting
    on my shoulder   all thru   all the talk about football and
one thing and another   it's listening   for my friend
to tell me about Aurobindo's mother   Well not
Aurobindo's mother   Aurobindo's   Mother

the intelligent farmer

Can the intelligent farmer enter the fire circle?
Or even just get up to the point in the hills
where the sun moon and stars playground
tilts down thru the clouds its axis angled
toward the ground?
I come
smelling around this fire—tho the best singing
is here I followed here
by nose. I hunt and I gather
by nose and by ear.
Just now
lovin'
enters by eye. I abdicate
all abdication of love all the time I watch the stars
gesturing.

There is a confluence of white smoke and dark smoke rising.
I can't tell if the two streams are embracing or wrestling
But they're going at it either way.

Klyd Watkins

speculation on first task

Soul is formless I hear   Then I guess
the first order of business of
the newborn babe   me   you   once
breath begins   is coming to perceive
form   Well the very first
wd be   perceiving the blur
of
light everywhere   marred by
unfocussed multiple parent forms
sorted by color more than line and by line more
than shape   There's a lot of eyeball
experimentation
has to happen to dial in
human form   Don't you guess?   Human forms
smiling down in adoration   Could be
just as our little knees and feet
find they can move.

I believe

I believe it doesn't too much matter what I believe
what matters is what I imagine
I believe watering a thirsty plant is better than thinking something unless
what you are thinking
loops you back around where you are drinking the blessing back from
the plant's drinking and a beneficial current encirculates among yall

I am certain the cessation of circumcision both male and female
sweetens the earth several
degrees   Think if we cd rescind circumcision wipe it out in retrospect
 there never have been
any   the flood of wise joy that wd wave over us and over us
I believe we can take from that   take wise joy   from the wild joy
imagined   breathe it

I believe it is immoral to write poetry that is not earthly   that is not
earthy   Guard against it
I don't know what to believe about the question can you lie on behalf of
the truth   That
has been my game   from time to time   I must say   I do think it's fun   I
guess we cd
ask the muse   Yes that's it   I believe we should ask the muse
before we decide in a particular poem
whether the picture there has to tell the truth
Should it not be allowed in some cases the kind of lying that is a making
the kind of lying that is creating what we are seeing

the kind of lying that makes the kind of space where
for some squiggly little truths   it's the only place at all
they could ever
appear?

I believe like a pastor shaking hands at the door with everyone
in the congregation as they leave, love will get around to us all
We will be astonished!   I didn't know I was going to get this!   Me?!

I don't believe we need to be reminded to polish our sorrow

I believe sometimes the best smile is no smile   That well-dressed
woman has enough to handle
without having to bother with forgiving some wounded male animal
for seeing she is beautiful

I'm pretty sure it takes more than one drop of rain
to make a flower grow   And I apologize
for that snarl in Elvis's voice when he sings that

I believe belief forgets it is in a tennis match
against Venus and Serena at the same time   I believe
belief has to make appointments to give news conferences
to sometimes tell us things but we need constant council

I believe I tease you about my belief while I ride the paradox camel

I bet Atheists   god love them   have as much trouble staying Atheists
as Christians have staying Christians   or Sikhs staying Sikhs or
what have you

The Wolf Can Smell This is My Acre

I mean in all the moving of the mind in its darkness when there's no
    accounting of the thinking

I believe a modest omnieloquent cellular jukebox shd pay for our drinks
    this evening
I believe I believe the most naïve are close to as smart as we are
I believe there is a monkey in the grass with his new guitar   his new guitar

confessional couplet

I am everything and nothing both so I get no credit
for my poems. But the wolf can smell this is my acre.

About the Author

Klyd Watkins has lived most of his life in Tennessee, except for teaching through the seventies at Madisonville Community College in Kentucky. He has also worked as a realtor and a honky tonk country bass player.

He and his wife Linda live now on the Harpeth River near White Bluff, with three of their four sons living nearby (the fourth is in LA, working for Disney). His five grandchildren are scattered around the country, but all three of his great-grandchildren live next door, making it convenient for him to attend their ball games.

He started publishing poetry throughout the late sixties and seventies in regional poetry magazines such as *Red Clay Reader*, *Southern Poetry Review* and *Poem*. His first publication was in *The Fisk Herald*. During the seventies, he interrupted his writing to make poetry on tape recorders, working alone and doing simultaneous improvisations with Linda, and with Peter and Particia Harleman, and with Toby and Ginny Tate. This work appeared on the series of lp's called *Poetry Out Loud* (numbers one through ten) and on the CD, *One Foot in the Garden*. The availability of recording equipment around the house stimulated his sons, who all became accomplished musicians.

He was active in the Nashville open mic scene back in the days of The Windows on the Cumberland readings and in C Ra McGuirt's "Dreadful House" salon. Nashville poet Joe Spears fortuitously suggested he submit to Charles Potts's *The Temple,* the Walla Walla, Washington poetry magazine and publishing complex, where he would publish frequently over the years. Eventually his collection *The Wind is Sacred There: a Journal of Radnor Lake* was published by Potts's press, Hand to Mouth.

Fresh inspiration from the move in 2017 from Nashville to the land on the Harpeth produced the poetry in this book.

Acknowledgments

Several of these poems appeared previously in the publications listed below.

Never Sent, "The Composition"

Salt, a Nashville multiformat zine, published "Serious Valentine," "at Willis's baseball practice at the park in Pegram," "Four Flows," and "Cottonwood Seed."

TimeBarn Produce I: feathers, "Miracles, " "hammock hoi dia 3 '22," "Nature Poem."

The Country Fried Panda Fest Poetry Anthology, "I Believe."

The chapbook *Spirit Trough* contains the poems (and one or two more) in the section herein of the same name. It was self published (TimeBarn Press is my imprint) in an edition of twenty-five copies.

The section of the current book called *Roy Acuff and Charley Pride talk about the Atlanta Braves on the stage of the Grand Ole Opry and other scenes*, along with a few more, were in the chapbook of the same name published by Hand to Mouth Press of Walla Walla, in an edition of one hundred copies.

www.ingramcontent.com/pod-product-compliance
Lightning Source LLC
Chambersburg PA
CBHW011222120626
46545CB00010B/3114